PHI

D0409918

WITHDRAWN

THE
PAUL HAMLYN
LIBRARY

———•———

DONATED BY

THE PAUL HAMLYN

FOUNDATION

TO THE

BRITISH MUSEUM

———•———

opened December 2000

14 Nov '06

Katharine
Hoare

THE BRITISH MUSEUM **Pocket Dictionary**

Kings & Queens of Britain

Katharine
Hoare

THE BRITISH MUSEUM PRESS

THE BRITISH MUSEUM
THE PAUL HAMLYN LIBRARY
WITHDRAWN

941.0099 HOA

© 2006 The Trustees of the British Museum

Published in 2006 by British Museum Press
A division of British Museum Company Ltd,
38 Russell Square, London, WC1B 3QQ

ISBN-13: 978-0-7141-3117-7
ISBN-10: 0-7141-3117-2

Katharine Hoare has asserted her right
to be identified as the author of this work.

A catalogue record for this title is
available from the British Library.

Designed and typeset by
HERRING BONE DESIGN
Printed and bound in Singapore

All photographs are taken by the British
Museum Photography and Imaging
Department, the British Museum, and
are © the Trustees of the British Museum,
except page 12 top: © Angelo
Hornak/Corbis.

Further information about the objects
illustrated in this book can be found at
www.thebritishmuseum.ac.uk/compass

CONTENTS

DYNASTIC LIST OF KINGS AND QUEENS

Introduction

Kings and queens have ruled in Britain for over a thousand years. The current queen is head of state for the United Kingdom and the Commonwealth (countries which were part of the British Empire but now have their own governments). The modern British monarchy is a constitutional monarchy. This means that the monarch is head of state while the government is run by a prime minister with the support of an elected parliament.

The role of the monarch has changed over time. Not only have there been struggles between different ruling families (known as dynasties) to wear the crown, but there have also been changes in the balance of power between the monarchs and their subjects – particularly the representatives of the people, who sit in parliament.

Elizabeth I was a member of the famous Tudor dynasty who ruled England in the sixteenth century.

The Roman emperor Hadrian (reigned 117–38), who visited the province of Britain.

The role of the monarch probably developed from the idea of a single person acting as the leader of a community. Early British monarchs ruled over their own independent kingdoms until AD 43, when Britain came under the control of the Roman empire. During the Roman period Britain was ruled by the Roman emperor, who appointed governors to rule the province of Britain on his behalf.

After the Romans left around AD 410, Britain again divided into small kingdoms. Some of these kingdoms grew more powerful than others, such as the kingdom of East Anglia whose king, Raedwald, was declared Bretwalda (sole ruler of Britain) in 616. During the ninth century the kings of Wessex became dominant, and during his lifetime Alfred of Wessex was referred to as the king of the English. Then, in 924, Alfred's grandson Athelstan of Wessex was crowned the first king of England by the Archbishop of Canterbury and the idea of one monarch for the whole country was established.

King Eadbald of Kent (reigned 616–40).

Rings made for the royal house of Wessex. The ring on the left is inscribed with the name of King Aethelwulf (reigned 839–56) while that on the right has the name of his daughter Aethelswith scratched onto the back. Aethelwulf was the father of Alfred the Great.

The British monarchy has developed out of a changing relationship between the rulers of the different regions of Britain. The current monarch is queen of England, Wales, Scotland and Northern Ireland, but this has not always been the case.

Wales only came under the complete authority of the English crown during the reign of Henry VIII (1509–47). Before this, Wales had its own kings and princes who were often in conflict with the English monarchs attempting to control the region. Scotland was ruled by its own monarch until 1603, when James VI of Scotland became king of England as well (as James I) and the two crowns combined. In Ireland, the English crown began by controlling the land around Dublin. In 1272 King Henry II titled himself Lord of Ireland, and then in 1541 the parliament in this area declared Henry VIII king of Ireland. This title lasted until 1801, when Ireland and Great Britain became the United Kingdom of Great Britain and Ireland. In 1949 southern Ireland became an independent republic, while Northern Ireland remained part of the United Kingdom.

The British monarch was also the ruler of land controlled by Britain in other parts of the world. This land was previously known as the British Empire. Today, countries with their own government who have the British monarch as their head of state are part of the Commonwealth of Nations.

Porcelain figure of George III. During George's reign the United States of America became independent and was no longer ruled by the British crown.

George I (left) who was succeeded by his eldest son George II (right) and Queen Caroline (seated).

His most Sacred Majesty King George & their Royal Highness's the Prince & Princess of Wales &c.

In Britain the title of king or queen passes from the monarch to his or her eldest surviving son (or the eldest daughter if there are no sons). If a monarch dies without any surviving children, the crown can pass across to a brother, sister or cousin, or down to a nephew, niece or grandchild. Sometimes different members of the royal family will compete for the crown, leading to conflict between the rival claimants and sometimes civil war. Civil war can also break out between monarch and subjects. This usually happens when the monarch is thought to be ruling in a way that gives him or her too much power or when the monarch makes decisions that are generally unpopular.

The wife of a king is usually known as the queen, although the husband of a queen does not automatically become a king. For example, Mary II's husband William of Orange was made joint monarch with Mary and became King William III, but Queen Victoria's husband Albert was given the title of Prince Consort and was never known as King Albert.

Raedwald
King of East Anglia *c.*593–625

Gold belt buckle from Sutton Hoo.

Raedwald, son of Tytila, King of East Anglia, became king in around 593. Following a number of battles with neighbouring kingdoms, Raedwald also became Bretwalda (overlord of the English kingdoms) from 616 until his death in 625. Raedwald was followed on the throne of East Anglia by his brother Eni and later his son Eorpwald and his step-son Sigebert.

Raedwald ruled at a time when Christianity was spreading across England. Raedwald himself became a Christian, though he continued to follow pagan beliefs as well and had both a Christian altar and a pagan shrine at his temple in Suffolk. Raedwald was probably buried at Sutton Hoo in a ship covered by a mound of soil. At the centre of this ship burial was a wooden chamber hung with textiles, where Raedwald's body was placed with weapons and armour, gold jewellery, silver vessels, drinking horns and musical instruments, and piles of clothes (linen shirts, woollen cloaks and fur trimmed caps).

Clasp from the Sutton Hoo purse which originally contained gold coins.

Alfred the Great

King of Wessex 870–99

Silver penny from the reign of Alfred.

Alfred was the fifth son of Aethelwulf, King of Wessex. He came to the throne after each of his elder brothers had been king in turn before him. Alfred married Eahlswith, a noblewoman from the kingdom of Mercia. He was followed as king by his son Edward the Elder.

During the ninth century, Danish Vikings settled in eastern England. From 870 they moved west and invaded Wessex in 878. Alfred defeated the Danes in battle and established a frontier dividing England in two. The north and east came under Danish control (Danelaw) while Alfred controlled West Mercia, Kent and Wessex from his palace at Winchester. To defend his lands Alfred strengthened the army and navy. He also built fortified settlements and reorganized local administration in the territory he controlled. He encouraged learning by having books on history, philosophy and religion translated from Latin into the Anglo-Saxon language. Alfred assembled existing laws, and added his own regulations, to form a single law code. By the 890s, royal documents and coins called Alfred 'king of the English'. His successors continued to extend Wessex's power, leading to a unified England under one monarch.

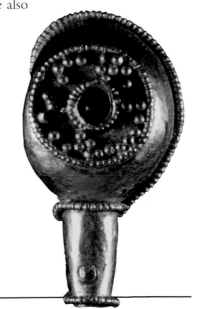

Gold fitting from the end of a pointer used as a guide when reading manuscripts.

William I

reigned 1066–87

William, son of Robert, Duke of Normandy, became duke when his father died in 1035 and was proclaimed king of England in 1066. William married Matilda of Flanders and they had ten children. On his death, William left Normandy to his eldest son Robert, his second son William succeeded as king of England, and the third son Henry was left £5000 in silver.

The Tower of London. Construction of the Tower began during William I's reign.

The last Saxon king of England was Harold II (a distant cousin of William I). William said that the previous king – Edward the Confessor – had promised him the throne. In September 1066 William crossed the Channel with a large army and defeated Harold at the Battle of Senlac (near Hastings) on 14 October. William was crowned king in Westminster Abbey on Christmas Day 1066. It took William six years to gain complete control over his new kingdom. To help with this he built over eighty stone castles and ordered a survey of land ownership which was recorded in the Domesday Book.

Detail from a carved ivory comb showing a figure dressed in the armour of a Norman soldier.

William II
reigned 1087–1100

Henry I
reigned 1100–1135

William II reigned for three years before dying in a hunting accident in the New Forest. He never married and was followed by his younger brother, Henry. Henry married twice. He and his first wife Edith had two children. His second wife Adela had no children. In 1120 Henry's son William drowned in a shipwreck. His daughter Matilda became heir to the throne, although on Henry's death his nephew Stephen succeeded as king.

William II continued to extend royal Norman authority over the north of England, and also took control of Normandy in France from his brother Robert. William's relations with the Church were not good and he had many arguments with the leader of the English church, the Archbishop of Canterbury.

Henry I centralized the administration of England and Normandy in the royal court. He spent time in both parts of his kingdom and used advisers to rule on his behalf when he was away. Henry increased royal revenues and established peaceful relations with Scotland by marrying Edith, daughter of the king of Scotland, in 1100. At her coronation as queen, Edith took the name Matilda, a fashionable Norman name.

Stone capital from Lewes Priory showing a scene from a story in the Bible.

13

Stephen
reigned 1135–54

Henry II
reigned 1154–1189

Stephen, a grandson of William I, became monarch instead of Henry I's daughter Matilda. Stephen and his wife (also called Matilda) had five children. Stephen was succeeded by Henry, son of his cousin Matilda. Henry and his wife, Eleanor of Aquitaine, had eight children. Henry was followed by his son Richard.

Stephen spent most of his reign defending his throne against his cousin Matilda, who believed she should be Queen. Matilda invaded England in 1139, and civil war broke out between the two sides. Matilda finally retired to Normandy in 1148, leaving Stephen to reign unopposed.

Altar plaque showing Henry of Blois, Bishop of Winchester, who was a firm supporter of his brother Stephen against Matilda.

Henry II ruled over England, Normandy and Aquitaine in France. He was interested in law and improved trials by using juries and sending judges around the country to try cases. Henry's relations with the Church were poor and he quarrelled with his friend Thomas à Becket, who had become Archbishop of Canterbury, leading to Becket's murder in 1170.

This object is called a reliquary. It was made to hold precious things associated with Thomas à Becket.

Richard I
reigned 1189–99

John
reigned 1199–1216

Richard was the third son of Henry II. Richard and his wife Berengaria had no children so Richard was succeeded by his brother John. John married twice. He had five children with his second wife Isabella, and his eldest son Henry followed him as king.

King Richard spent a lot of time away from England. In 1190, he left to lead an army in the religious wars known as the Crusades. Later, on his way back to England, Richard was captured in Austria and held prisoner. In Richard's absence, his brother John tried to make himself king. However, Richard was released in 1194, and re-crowned at Winchester.

King John was interested in improving the law and government but heavy taxes, arguments with the Church and unsuccessful wars in France made him unpopular. Many of his nobles rebelled, and in June 1215 they made John sign an agreement, known as Magna Carta, which limited royal powers. John tried to ignore these restrictions on his authority, and civil war broke out between the king and his nobles in 1216. John died later the same year.

Glazed tile showing Richard I (left) and his opponent Saladin (right) in the Third Crusade.

Henry III

reigned 1216–72

Wall painting of a biblical prophet from Westminster Palace.

Henry III was only nine when he became king, and the country was ruled on his behalf by a group of nobles until 1227. Henry and his wife Eleanor of Provence had five children. Henry was followed as king by his eldest son Edward.

Henry III made many charitable donations and spent money on building works, including the rebuilding of Westminster Abbey. This meant high taxes to raise money. These taxes, together with his failed campaigns in France and his choice of advisers, made him unpopular and the nobles attempted to limit royal power by setting up a council to help rule the country. However, in 1262 Henry rejected these arrangements and civil war broke out. In 1265 Henry eventually defeated the nobles, who were led by Simon de Montfort. Royal authority was restored and the king promised to uphold the Magna Carta.

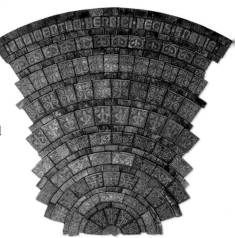

Floor tiles from Clarendon Palace in Wiltshire. The palace was refurbished by Henry III.

Edward I
reigned 1272–1307

This bronze jug in the shape of a mounted knight was used to pour water for hand-washing during meals.

Edward I was named after the Anglo-Saxon king, Edward the Confessor. He married Eleanor of Castile and they had thirteen children. After Eleanor's death Henry married Margaret of France. Edward was succeeded by his eldest surviving son, also called Edward.

Edward I was determined to extend his authority across Britain. Wales was brought into the English legal system, a network of castles was built to control the region and Edward's young son was proclaimed the first English Prince of Wales in 1301. When Queen Margaret of Scotland died in 1290 without an heir, Edward chose John Balliol as the next king. However, Balliol quarrelled with the Scottish nobles and left Scotland, so Edward appointed three Englishmen to run Scotland. In 1304, following a rebellion led by William Wallace, a council was set up to govern Scotland. Two years later one council member, Robert the Bruce, rebelled against English control and was crowned king of Scotland. Edward led an army northward to fight the Scots but died on the way.

A thirteenth-century gold brooch set with rubies and sapphires.

Edward II
reigned 1307–27

Edward II was the son of Edward I. He and his wife, Isabella of France, had four children. Following civil war with the English nobles, Edward was forced to abdicate in favour of his son who became Edward III. Edward II was later murdered at Berkeley Castle.

A seal used on official documents. It was issued by the Scottish monastery depicted on the seal.

Edward II liked to rule with the advice and support of a few close friends. The nobles felt excluded and throughout Edward's reign they tried to gain more power. In 1311, they attempted to limit the king's control of finance and appointments, but were ignored by Edward. Edward built up large debts and was defeated in 1314 at the Battle of Bannockburn by the Scottish king, Robert the Bruce. In 1321, civil war broke out between Edward and his nobles, who were supported by his wife Isabella. In 1326 Edward was captured in Wales and in January 1327 he was forced to resign the throne. His young son Edward was proclaimed king in his place.

The lid of this casket is decorated with the personal emblems of Edward II's family. The emblems on the front of the lid belong to Isabella of France, who married Edward in 1308. Those on the other side belong to Edward's stepmother Margaret, who was the second wife of Edward I.

Edward III

reigned 1327–77

A portrait of Edward III from a coin.

Edward III became king at the age of fourteen when his father abdicated. At first Edward's mother helped him rule but in 1330 he became sole ruler. Edward married Philippa of Hainault and they had twelve children. He was followed as king by his grandson Richard.

Edward III decided to extend his kingdom and took an army to claim the French crown. He defeated the French king, Philip VI, at the Battle of Crécy and by 1360 controlled over a quarter of France. However, in 1375, the French king, Charles V, won back most of this land leaving Edward Calais and the land near Bordeaux. Conflict between England and France continued for many years and became known as the Hundred Years' War. Edward's reign saw several outbreaks of the Black Death plague which killed many people, including one of the king's daughters. The plague caused an economic crisis and laws were introduced to control wages and prices.

An embroidered panel showing scenes from the life of the Virgin Mary. The figures are shown wearing fourteenth-century clothes.

Richard II

reigned 1377–99

Edward III's eldest son died in 1376, leaving Edward's grandson Richard as heir to the throne. Richard was ten years old when he became king, and England was ruled by a council led by his uncle John of Gaunt. Richard married Anne of Bohemia and then Isabella of France. He had no children. In 1399, Richard's cousin Henry deposed him and Richard was later killed in Pontefract Castle.

Edward III's eldest son was known as the Black Prince. He died in 1376 and this badge commemorates his funeral.

Richard's reign saw a long truce in the Hundred Years' War with France. In 1381 a rebellion known as the Peasants' Revolt broke out. The king met the rebels at Smithfield, London and their leader, Wat Tyler, was captured. Richard's authoritarian manner and his reliance on a few friends led to criticism by parliament. Richard banished many of his opponents, including his cousin Henry of Bolingbroke, who later returned and claimed the crown for himself.

This jug, marked with the royal coat of arms and Richard II's personal emblem the white hart, was made in England and later taken to Africa.

Henry IV

reigned 1399–1413

Henry IV was the son of John of Gaunt, Duke of Lancaster, and a grandson of Edward III. Henry quarrelled with his cousin Richard II and in 1399 captured Richard and declared himself king. Henry and his first wife Mary de Bohun had six children. In 1402 Henry married again to Joan of Navarre. Henry was succeeded by his eldest son, also called Henry.

Not everybody agreed that Henry IV should be king and in 1400 there was a revolt in Wales led by Owen Glendower. In early July 1403 Henry's former supporters, the Percys of Northumberland, turned against him and raised an army in Cheshire in opposition to his rule. Henry IV's army, under the command of his eldest son, marched to meet the rebels and defeated them in battle on 21 July just outside Shrewsbury. By 1408 Henry had gained complete control of his kingdom. From 1405 onwards Henry suffered from ill health and his eldest son began to take more of a role in government, even opposing his father at times.

The swan was the personal emblem of Henry's first wife Mary de Bohun and was used by supporters of the House of Lancaster.

Henry V
reigned 1413–22

Henry VI
reigned 1422–61, 1470–71

Henry V, eldest son of Henry IV, married Katherine of France. When Henry died his one-year-old son succeeded him. Henry VI married Margaret of Anjou. Their only son was killed in battle in 1471. Henry VI was deposed by Edward of York and died in the Tower of London.

Henry V spent a lot of time fighting in France. In 1415, he won the Battle of Agincourt and gained control of Normandy. He was interested in music and gave pensions to court composers.

Henry VI's reign began with his uncles ruling on his behalf. Only later did he reign by himself. Henry was interested in education and founded Eton School and King's College, Cambridge. In 1453, the king fell ill and Richard, Duke of York, was made Protector. Henry recovered but civil war broke out (the Wars of the Roses) between the king's Lancastrian supporters and the Yorkist supporters of the duke. Henry was imprisoned and Edward (the Duke of York's son) became king. Henry was restored in 1470, although Edward regained the throne the next year.

A carved panel showing a biblical scene with people dressed in fifteenth-century clothing.

Edward IV
reigned 1461–70, 1471–83

Edward V
reigned 1483

Edward IV, son of the Duke of York and Cicely Neville, was descended from Edward III. He married Elizabeth Woodville and they had ten children. When Edward died, his twelve-year-old son became king with his uncle, Richard Duke of Gloucester, as Protector. Edward V only reigned for two months before his uncle had him and his younger brother Richard imprisoned in the Tower of London. Richard declared himself king and the young Edward V was never seen again.

Edward IV took a strong personal interest in government. He sat in person to enforce justice, introduced strict management of royal revenues to reduce the Crown's debt, encouraged trade and made peace with France. Edward collected illuminated manuscripts but also supported the new invention of printing.

Edward V was never crowned king. As he was travelling to London for his coronation, his uncle seized the throne and Edward was deposed.

This jewellery was probably buried for safekeeping during the Wars of the Roses.

Richard III

reigned 1483–85

Richard, Duke of Gloucester, was Edward IV's brother. When Edward died, Richard became Protector for his young nephew Edward V but soon made himself king instead. Richard III's only son died while he was king and Richard himself was killed in battle by Henry Tudor, who took the throne as Henry VII.

Richard attempted to rebuild relations with Lancastrian supporters by showing consideration to Lancastrians punished by Edward IV and moving Henry VI's body to St George's Chapel at Windsor. The first laws written entirely in English were passed during his reign. Before becoming king, Richard had many supporters in the north of England and this led to resentment in the south. In 1485, Henry Tudor (a distant cousin of Richard III) landed in Wales to claim the throne. On 22 August, at Bosworth in Leicestershire, Henry's forces defeated Richard's army and Richard was killed.

The boar was Richard III's emblem and thousands of boar badges were made as souvenirs of Richard's coronation in 1483.

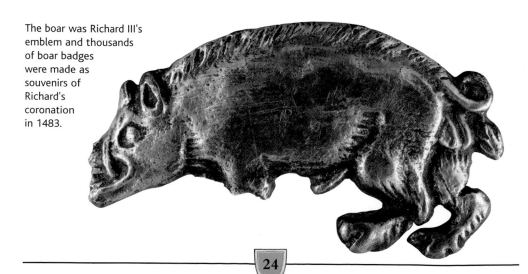

Henry VII

reigned 1485–1509

Henry Tudor was descended from Edward III through John of Gaunt, Duke of Lancaster. After defeating Richard III at the Battle of Bosworth, Henry declared himself king and married Elizabeth of York, the eldest daughter of Edward IV. Henry and Elizabeth had seven children. Henry was succeeded by his second son Henry.

Henry's early reign was troubled by revolts involving claimants to the throne pretending to be Edward V or his brother. Henry united the Lancastrians and Yorkists by marrying Elizabeth of York and used royal marriages to maintain peace abroad. One daughter, Margaret, married James IV of Scotland (from whom Mary, Queen of Scots and her son, James VI of Scotland and I of England, were descended) and his other daughter, Mary, married Louis XII of France. Henry increased royal income and left a full treasury on his death. Although Henry called seven Parliaments during his reign, they had little influence on national events and policies.

A glass flask decorated with a portrait of Henry VII. The flask was made in Italy and was probably given to Henry as a diplomatic gift by an Italian duke in 1506.

Henry VIII

reigned 1509–47

Gold medal showing Henry VIII.

Henry VIII was the second son of Henry VII. He became heir to the throne after the death of his brother Arthur. Henry married Arthur's widow Katherine of Aragon and they had one daughter, Mary. Henry had five further wives – Anne Boleyn, Jane Seymour, Anne of Cleves, Catherine Howard and Katharine Parr – and two more children, Elizabeth and Edward. All his children reigned in turn after his death.

As a young king, Henry was athletic and enjoyed writing and playing music. Henry's lack of interest in government business increased the influence of his Lord Chancellor, Thomas Wolsey, who also became a cardinal in 1515. Henry was keen to increase England's power abroad and he expanded the size of the navy from five to fifty-three ships. He attempted to invade France several times, though in the end only the town of Boulogne was captured. The cost of these wars led to inflation in England.

A chalk drawing of women at the royal court by the artist Hans Holbein.

This small prayer book, with a decorated gold cover, was made to be worn on a lady's belt.

The second half of Henry's reign was dominated by the Protestant Reformation, which led to the foundation of the Church of England. Henry wanted a son to follow him as king but he and his wife, Katherine of Aragon, had only one daughter. Meanwhile, Henry had fallen in love with Anne Boleyn, one of the ladies at the royal court attending Queen Katherine. Wolsey tried to persuade the Pope to allow Henry to end his marriage to Katherine and marry Anne instead. He failed, and was dismissed from power. Henry's next chief minister, Thomas Cromwell, used Parliament to pass a series of laws that reduced the Pope's power and made Henry the head of the Church in England. At the same time, monastic lands and possessions belonging to the Roman Catholic Church were sold during what is known as the Dissolution of the Monasteries.

Henry divorced Katherine and married Anne in 1533. They had one daughter, Elizabeth. Henry married four more times and had one more child, a son named Edward, with his third wife Jane Seymour. Henry's will set up a Council of Regents, consisting of sixteen nobles, to help the young Edward to rule after his father's death.

A portrait of Henry VIII from the end of his reign, when he was married to his sixth wife, Katharine Parr.

Edward VI
reigned 1547–53

Edward VI was the only child of Henry VIII and Jane Seymour. He became king at the age of nine and reigned for six years. Edward made Lady Jane Grey (a great-granddaughter of Henry VII) his heir but she only reigned for nine days before Edward's sister, Mary, claimed the crown.

During Edward's reign England became more Protestant. Religious statues and stained glass were removed from churches, clergy were allowed to marry and a new Book of Common Prayer replaced Latin services with English. Because of his young age, Edward ruled with the help of a council, the president of which was his uncle Edward Seymour. In 1551 Seymour was replaced by the Duke of Northumberland, who married his son to Lady Jane Grey and persuaded Edward to make Jane his heir.

When Edward died in 1553, Jane was declared queen by the council. However, Edward's sister Mary gathered an army and marched to London where she successfully claimed the crown. Jane was imprisoned in the Tower and executed in 1554.

Portrait of Edward VI from a gold medal celebrating his coronation.

Mary I
reigned 1553–58

Gold coin from the reign of Mary I.

Mary I, daughter of Henry VIII and Katherine of Aragon, was the first queen to reign in her own right rather than being a queen because she was married to a king. She came to the throne following the death of her brother Edward. Mary married King Philip II of Spain. They had no children and Mary was succeeded by her younger sister Elizabeth.

Mary was a Roman Catholic and she tried to return England to the Roman Catholic faith. She made the Pope head of the Church again, encouraged the return of monastic orders and had followers of the Protestant faith arrested. This made Mary very unpopular and she was unable to convert her subjects back to Roman Catholicism. Mary's marriage to Philip of Spain involved England in a war with France during which Calais, the last area of France controlled by England, was recaptured by the French.

Portrait of Mary from an illustrated scroll of English monarchs made during her sister Elizabeth's reign.

Elizabeth I

reigned 1558–1603

Elizabeth I was the daughter of King Henry VIII and his second wife Anne Boleyn. Her younger brother Edward and her older sister Mary sat on the throne before her. Both died without leaving children, so the throne eventually passed to Elizabeth. Elizabeth chose not to marry and at the end of her forty-five-year reign she was succeeded by King James VI of Scotland, the son of her second cousin Mary, Queen of Scots.

This gold medal was probably a gift for one of Elizabeth's favourite courtiers.

This velvet purse was used to store the Great Seal of England, which was used on important official documents.

The Tudor period was a time of great religious change in England. Elizabeth's father, Henry VIII, had changed the official religion of the country from Roman Catholic to Protestant and the reigns of Edward and Mary saw religious conflict between these two religious groups. During Elizabeth's reign the power of the Protestant church was strengthened and the Church of England – with Elizabeth at its head – was officially established.

During Elizabeth's reign English influence in Ireland increased, and voyages of exploration to America were undertaken by Walter Raleigh and Francis Drake. At the same time England was often threatened with invasion by her European neighbours France and Spain. In 1588 the Spanish king Philip II sent a fleet of about 130 ships, known as the Armada, to invade England. There was a great naval battle between the Spanish and the English which ended in victory for the English navy.

A golden pendant with a portrait of Elizabeth I.

Elizabeth was keen to promote her position as queen across the whole of her kingdom. She commissioned many portraits showing her as a powerful ruler dressed in expensive clothes and jewellery. She also undertook tours around her kingdom. These were known as progresses and they gave Elizabeth an opportunity to visit some of the most powerful families in the country and to be seen by people beyond London, where her court was based.

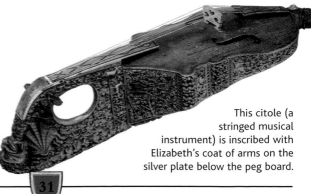

The famous playwright William Shakespeare. Several of his plays were first performed at court in front of Queen Elizabeth I.

This citole (a stringed musical instrument) is inscribed with Elizabeth's coat of arms on the silver plate below the peg board.

James I (VI of Scotland)
reigned 1603–25 (king of Scotland from 1567)

Miniature portrait of James I.

James I was the great-great-grandson of Henry VII. James became king of Scotland in 1567 and king of England thirty-six years later on the death of Elizabeth I. He married Anne of Denmark and they had seven children. James died in 1625 having ruled Scotland for fifty-eight years and England for twenty-two years.

James, as head of the Church of England, ordered a new translation of the Bible in 1604. Known as the Authorised King James Version, it was published in 1611. In 1605, Roman Catholic conspirators (including Guy Fawkes) tried to blow up Parliament – a conspiracy which became known as the Gunpowder Plot. James was a keen scholar, who supported science, art and literature, and employed the architect Inigo Jones to improve royal buildings. As a firm believer in royal authority, James was often in dispute with Parliament. One Parliament lasted only eight weeks, and when James summoned Parliament in 1621 to raise taxes, the House of Commons demanded to discuss any subject they thought was important, so James dissolved it. During most of his reign, the leading Catholic and Protestant countries in Europe were involved in the Thirty Years' War, but Britain did not actively take part until after James' death.

A playing card showing Guy Fawkes being questioned by James I and his council.

Guy Fawkes brought to ỹ Council where he laments nothing but ỹ he had not Executed his designe

Charles I
reigned 1625–49

Interregnum
1649–60

Charles I on horseback.

Charles I, second son of James I, succeeded to the thrones of England and Scotland in 1625. He married Henrietta Maria of France and they had nine children. Following civil war between the king and Parliament, Charles was executed and England became a republic. Charles's eldest son was crowned King Charles II in 1660.

Charles often argued with Parliament about financial and religious matters – particularly unpopular taxes and a new Prayer Book for Scotland. In 1642, these disagreements led to civil war. A number of battles were fought but it was not until 1648 that Parliament, under Oliver Cromwell, defeated the Royalist army.

Charles was beheaded in January 1649 and England became a republic under Cromwell. This period is known as the Interregnum, which means 'between reigns'. Cromwell disagreed with Parliament over the constitution, control of the army and religious toleration so in 1653 Parliament was dissolved and he became Lord Protector. After Cromwell's death, Parliament invited Charles I's son to become king.

A bust of Oliver Cromwell.

Charles II
reigned 1660–85

A gold medal showing
Charles II.

Charles II was the eldest son of Charles I. After his father lost the English Civil War Charles escaped to France where he remained until he was invited back to England to become king in 1660. He married Catherine of Braganza. They had no children and when he died in 1685 his brother James succeeded to the throne.

Charles II ruled with the support of a group of ministers who advised him about domestic and foreign policy. Charles also had to listen to Parliament's ideas about how the country should be run and sometimes had to change what he wanted to do if Parliament strongly disagreed with him.

Rivalry over trade and control of overseas territories led to war with the Dutch. The Dutch settlement at New Amsterdam in America was captured by the British and renamed New York. In 1667 England made peace with the Dutch, and the next year the two countries formed an alliance with the Swedish against the French, although Charles later made peace with the French king Louis XIV.

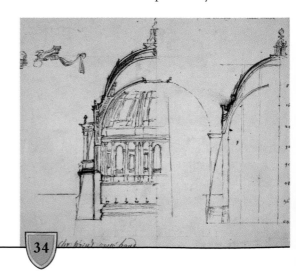

Christopher Wren's design for the dome of the new St Paul's cathedral. Work began on the cathedral in 1675 but it was not completed until 1710.

POTENTISSIMO AC SERENISSIMO CAROLO II DEI GRATIA MAGNÆ BRITANNIÆ FRANCIÆ ET HIBERNIÆ REGI FIDEI DEFENSORI. etc.

Charles II on horseback.

Throughout Charles's reign, there was much debate in Parliament about religion. Charles himself was sympathetic to the Roman Catholic faith while Parliament supported the Protestant Church of England and tried to prevent Charles's Roman Catholic brother James from becoming king after Charles. Charles eventually dissolved Parliament to prevent them passing an exclusion Bill against James and ruled for the last five years of his reign without the support of Parliament.

In 1665 there was a serious outbreak of plague in London, which killed many people and forced the royal court to move to Oxford. This was followed in 1666 by the Great Fire of London, which destroyed many buildings. An eyewitness account of events during both the plague and the Great Fire was recorded by Samuel Pepys in his famous diary.

Charles II was a patron of Christopher Wren, who designed and rebuilt St Paul's Cathedral, Chelsea Hospital and many other buildings in the capital. Charles supported the founding of the Royal Society to promote scientific research and encouraged the building of the Greenwich Observatory.

A Delftware plate made in London in 1663.

James II
reigned 1685–9

James II.

James, second son of Charles I, became king when his elder brother died. James and his first wife, Anne Hyde, had two daughters while his second wife, Mary of Modena, had two sons and three daughters. James was deposed in 1688 and was succeeded by his eldest daughter Mary and her husband William. James died in France in 1701.

As Duke of York, James was appointed Lord High Admiral and commanded the Royal Navy during the wars with the Dutch. James became a Roman Catholic in 1669 and, as king, tried to support the Roman Catholic faith. He appointed Catholics to important academic, military and political posts and attempted to withdraw laws against Catholicism. This caused disagreements with Parliament so James dissolved Parliament and ruled without it.

In June 1688 James and his second wife Mary of Modena had a son, Charles Edward Stuart. Since James II and his wife were both Roman Catholic, it seemed likely that their son, the next king, would also be Roman Catholic. This was unpopular with James' subjects. A group of nobles appealed for help to the Protestant William of Orange, husband of James's daughter Mary. In November William invaded England and James fled to France. In 1689 James took a French army to Ireland to try to regain his crown, but he was defeated by William's forces at the Battle of the Boyne in 1690. James spent the rest of his life in exile in France.

William III and Mary II

reigned 1689–1702

Mary II was the elder daughter of James II and Anne Hyde. She married her cousin, William of Orange. They had no children. Mary died in 1694 and William continued to reign until his death in 1702. He was succeeded by Anne, the second daughter of James II.

In 1689, Parliament declared that James had abdicated by leaving his kingdom the previous year. William and Mary were offered the throne as joint monarchs. They were expected to summon Parliament frequently and listen to Parliament's decisions about new laws, taxes and the army. In 1696, William established a group of ministers who helped to decide government policies. Abroad, William wanted to prevent France from becoming too powerful and joined with the Dutch to fight France during the Nine Years' War. War was expensive and in 1694 the Bank of England was established to raise money.

A 1689 procession in honour of William and Mary.

Anne
reigned 1702–14

Glass engraved with
a portrait of
Queen Anne.

Anne was the second daughter of James II and
Anne Hyde. She married George, Prince of
Denmark. They had eighteen children but none
of them survived childhood. When William III
died, Anne became queen. After Anne the throne
passed to her distant cousin and the great-
grandson of James I, George of Hanover.

Military victories over France and Spain by John Churchill,
Duke of Marlborough, strengthened England's position in
Europe. Party politics became more significant with Whigs
(who supported limited
monarchy) and Tories
(who favoured strong
monarchy) competing
for power. Since James I
England and Scotland had
been ruled by one monarch, although each
country had its own parliament. In 1707, the
two Parliaments agreed to unite into one
British Parliament at Westminster. It was also
agreed that the two countries would have the
same flag and coinage, though Scotland kept
its own legal, education and Church systems.

Sir Hans Sloane was a doctor to Queen Anne. On his death
his collection of objects founded the British Museum.

George I
reigned 1714–27

George II
reigned 1727–69

The Act of Parliament which founded the British Museum in 1753.

George of Hanover inherited the throne in 1714. He and his wife Sophia had two children and when George died he was succeeded by his son. George II and his wife Caroline had eight children, though George's eldest son Frederick died before him, so the crown passed to his grandson George III.

George I spent much of his time in Hanover and depended on his ministers to help him rule England. The ministers held regular cabinet meetings and when Robert Walpole took over as leader of the Cabinet he became the first 'Prime Minister'.

Like his father, George II faced claims to the crown by James II's son and grandson, until their cause was finally defeated at the Battle of Culloden in 1746. George's reign saw increased production in coal mining, shipbuilding and agriculture, together with a rapid rise in population. Overseas trade also grew following military victories which gave England control of parts of India and Canada.

Bowl showing Charles Edward Stuart, grandson of James II, also known as the Young Pretender.

George III
reigned 1769–1820

George III was the first Hanoverian monarch to be born in England and to speak English as his first language (George I and II both spoke German). George III and his wife, Charlotte, had fifteen children. During the last ten years of his reign George became unwell and his eldest son, later King George IV, acted as Prince Regent and ruled the country on his father's behalf.

George was a conscientious ruler. He read government papers and took an interest in government policy although he had to listen to the views of his ministers before making decisions about economic, religious and foreign policy. One of the major events of his reign was the American declaration of independence from British rule in 1776. This established the United States of America as an independent country.

The Rosetta Stone was given to the British Museum in 1802 by George III. It dates from 196 BC and records a decree of the ancient Egyptian king Ptolemy V in three ancient scripts.

Portrait of George III dressed in ancient Roman costume.

George III was the first king to study science as part of his education and he had his own astronomical observatory. He also took a keen interest in agriculture and was nicknamed Farmer George. George owned a huge collection of books, 65,000 of which were later given to the British Museum to start a national library (now the British Library). He also gave objects to the British Museum, including some of the first objects in the ancient Egyptian collection.

In 1793 war broke out between Britain and France and continued for many years. In 1805 the Royal Navy under Nelson won a great victory over the French navy at the Battle of Trafalgar. The French emperor, Napoleon Bonaparte, was finally defeated at the Battle of Waterloo in 1815.

During his time in England, the composer Mozart and his family played for George III and visited the British Museum.

Paper collage of a lily made by Mary Delany. She became acquainted with George III and Queen Charlotte, who provided her with a house in Windsor towards the end of her life.

A porcelain mug decorated with a portrait of George III.

George IV

reigned 1820–30

George IV was the eldest son of George III. He ruled as Prince Regent from 1810 and became king ten years later. He married Princess Caroline of Brunswick in 1795. Sadly, their only child Charlotte died in childbirth. When George died he was succeeded by his brother William.

Gilt bronze medal showing George IV.

George IV was interested in art and architecture. He collected many important paintings, built the Royal Pavilion at Brighton and renovated Windsor Castle and Buckingham Palace. George was fond of pageants and parties and he ran up huge personal debts, which had to be paid off with grants voted to him by Parliament. He made royal visits to different parts of his kingdom including Hanover, Ireland and Scotland. In 1829 George IV agreed to Catholic Emancipation, which reduced religious discrimination against Roman Catholics.

William IV

reigned 1830–37

Indian silver coin from the reign of William IV.

William IV was the third son of George III. William served as an officer in the Royal Navy before becoming king when his brother George IV died. William married Princess Adelaide of Saxe-Meiningen in 1818 and had two daughters, both of whom died in infancy. William was followed on the throne by his niece Victoria.

The role of ordinary people in helping to decide government policy grew during William's reign. In 1832 the king signed the Great Reform Bill, which aimed to improve the way that members of Parliament were elected. New standardized rules saying who was allowed to vote in parliamentary elections were introduced and the right to vote was extended so that more people were able to decide who they wanted as their representative in Parliament.

Right: British Museum porter wearing the uniform issued by William IV in 1836.

Far right: Statue of King Ramesses II being moved into the new Egyptian gallery at the British Museum in 1834.

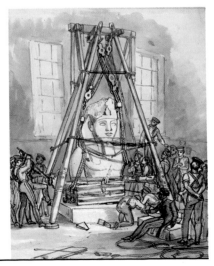

Victoria
reigned 1837–1901

Queen Victoria is the longest reigning British monarch. She became queen at the age of eighteen, following the death of her uncle William IV, and reigned for sixty-three years. She and her husband, Prince Albert, had nine children – five daughters and four sons. When

Scottish bank note showing Victoria and Albert.

Albert died in 1861, Victoria was devastated and wore mourning for the rest of her life. She was succeeded by her eldest son Edward.

Victoria's reign was a time of great industrial expansion and in 1842 Victoria became the first reigning monarch to travel by train. During the second half of her

Visitors to the British Museum in 1881 listening to a talk about ancient sculptures.

reign, Britain's empire in Africa and Asia increased in size and in 1877 Victoria was declared Empress of India. Victoria was a constitutional monarch. She had little direct power but was able to influence decisions made by her ministers, especially the Prime Minister. Famous Prime Ministers during her reign included Lord Melbourne, Benjamin Disraeli and Lord Gladstone.

Victoria was skilled at drawing and painting and throughout her life she kept a diary describing her family life and royal duties. As well as the existing royal palaces, Victoria bought Osborne House on the Isle of Wight as a family home in 1845. Albert bought Balmoral Castle, in Scotland, in 1852. Images of Victoria and her family were widely available through newspapers and the growing use of photography.

Badge made to celebrate Victoria's Diamond Jubilee in 1897. The idea for pin badges had been developed by an American company only a year before.

In 1854 Britain entered the Crimean War in support of the Turkish Ottoman Empire against Russia. During this conflict Florence Nightingale and Mary Seacole, working to help wounded British soldiers, developed the practice of modern nursing.

Victoria attended her last public function in 1899, when she laid the foundation stone for new buildings at the South Kensington Museum. The Museum had been established in 1852 with money raised during the Great Exhibition of 1851. It was later renamed the Victoria and Albert Museum in honour of the queen and her husband.

Photograph showing the Reading Room at the British Museum being built in 1855. The Reading Room took three years to build and still stands in the Great Court of the Museum.

Edward VII
reigned 1901–10

George V
reigned 1910–27

An ancient Egyptian-style brooch based on princess Alexandra's 'Thebes' brooch.

Edward was Victoria's eldest son. He married Princess Alexandra of Denmark and they had six children. George V, second son of Edward VII, served in the Royal Navy until his brother Albert died in 1892 making him heir to the throne. He married Mary of Teck and they had four sons and one daughter.

Edward VII's main interest lay in foreign affairs and he encouraged military and naval reforms to strengthen Britain's defences. He spoke fluent French and German and made a number of visits abroad.

In 1911 George V and Queen Mary travelled to India to attend celebrations in their honour. During the First World War (1914-18) George visited soldiers fighting in Europe and the wounded in hospital. In 1917, George changed the royal family's name to Windsor (after the Castle). Civil war in Ireland in support of Home Rule led to the formation of the Irish Free State (later the Irish Republic) in 1922. The six northern counties of Ireland remained part of the United Kingdom.

George V opening the King Edward VII Wing of the British Museum in 1914.

Edward VIII

reigned 1936

George VI

reigned 1936–52

Portrait of George IV, from a banknote.

Edward VIII, eldest son of George V, was king for only 325 days before he abdicated and his brother became King George VI. George married Lady Elizabeth Bowes-Lyon and they had two daughters. When George V died his elder daughter Elizabeth became Queen.

As Prince of Wales, Edward fell in love with Mrs Wallis Simpson. When he became king he had to choose between remaining king and marrying Mrs Simpson who, as a divorced woman, was not considered suitable to be queen. Edward decided to abdicate. He became the Duke of Windsor and married Wallis Simpson. At first the Duke lived in Europe before being appointed Governor of the Bahamas from 1940 until 1945. He continued to live abroad, making occasional visits to England, until his death in Paris in 1972.

As Duke of York, George served in both the Royal Navy and the Royal Air Force. Three years after be became king, the Second World War (1939–45) broke out. George VI remained in London throughout the war and formed a close working relationship with the wartime Prime Minister, Winston Churchill. After the war many countries such as India, which had been part of the British Empire, gained independence from British rule and formed their own governments. Towards the end of his reign, George VI became very unwell, and his daughter Princess Elizabeth took on many of his royal duties.

Elizabeth II
reigned 1952–

Elizabeth II.

Elizabeth II was born in London in 1926, the first child of the Duke and Duchess of York. When her father became king in 1936, Elizabeth, as his eldest daughter, became heir to the throne. She married Prince Philip of Greece (created Duke of Edinburgh in 1947) and they have a daughter and three sons. Her eldest son, Charles, is the current Prince of Wales and next in line to the throne.

Elizabeth II's coronation on 2 June 1953 took place at Westminster Abbey and was watched on television across Britain. The queen is currently head of state in sixteen countries around the world and she has made many royal visits both within Britain and abroad. As head of state in Britain, the queen holds regular meetings with the Prime Minister and formally opens Parliament each October. The queen is also the Supreme Governor of the Chursch of England, although in practice the Church is run by the Archbishop of Canterbury. A variety of world religions are followed in Britain today, and the queen has met with many leaders of these faiths. Elizabeth II continues the tradition, started by her grandfather George V in 1932, of delivering an annual Christmas broadcast to Britain and the Commonwealth. During her reign Elizabeth has celebrated two jubilees – her Silver Jubilee (twenty-five years on the throne) in 1977 and her Golden Jubilee (fifty years on the throne) in 2002.